Daily Confessions
for Parents, Husbands,
Wives and Teens

Other books in *The Successful Family* Series

Daily Confessions
for Parents, Husbands,
Wives and Teens

Dr. Creflo A. Dollar and Taffi L. Dollar

Daily Confessions for Parents, Husbands, Wives and Teens
ISBN 1-59089-725-0
Copyright © 2003 by Dr. Creflo A. Dollar and Taffi L. Dollar

Published by:
Creflo Dollar Ministries
P.O. Box 490124
College Park, GA 30349

CONTENTS

1

DAILY
CONFESSIONS FOR
PARENTS

Godly Parenting

- In the name of Jesus, I declare that I have the efficiency, ability and might to raise my children in the fear and admonition of the Lord (Acts 1:8, *AMP*).

- I will teach and impress the Word of God diligently on their minds and hearts (Deuteronomy 6:7, *AMP*).

- I declare that as I increase in the knowledge of God, I will raise my children according to His will. They walk worthy of the Lord and His calling on their lives. They live lives that are pleasing to Him and are fruitful in every good work (Colossians 1:9-10).

- I will live a life before my children that brings honor to God.

- I declare that the wisdom of God is in me and He directs my path regarding my children (Proverbs 3:6; Colossians 1:9, 3:16).

- The Lord will perfect that which concerns me. Therefore, He is perfecting every concern that I have for my children (Psalm 138:8).

- I cast all my cares concerning my children on God, because He cares for me (1 Peter 5:7; Psalm 55:22).

- I will not irritate or provoke my children to anger, but will rear them tenderly in the training, discipline, counsel and admonition of the Lord (Ephesians 6:4, *AMP*).

- I commit my children into God's care and am confident that He is able to finish the work that He has begun in their lives (Philippians 1:6).

- I am sensitive to the anointing that is on my children (Leviticus 7:36).

- I bind the hand of the enemy in any way that he comes to kill, steal or destroy in the lives of my children (Matthew 18:18; John 10:10). I loose the angels of God to go forth now to guard and protect my children.

Children's Overall Well-Being

- In the name of Jesus, I declare that my children are saved and serving the Lord (Joshua 24:15; Acts 16:31).

- I declare that my children obey me in all things according to God's Word and they please the Lord (Colossians 3:20).

- My children obey all those in authority over them for it is right in the sight of God (Ephesians 6:1-3).

- I believe that correction causes my children to be better in life (Proverbs 17:10). They do not refuse correction, but receive it gladly and continue in the things of God (Proverbs 10:17;15:10).

- My children love instruction and correction (Proverbs 12:1).

- I declare that my children follow God's path in this life.

- I thank You, Lord, that those who have authority over my children do not withhold correction from them. Strong correction will not cause them to die or become depressed, but will instead deliver them from destruction (Proverbs 23:13-14).

- I declare that my children are anointed because they obey God and keep all of His commandments (Deuteronomy 11:27).

- No corrupt communication proceeds out of the mouths of my children.

- I declare that my children are mighty and powerful people on the earth (Psalm 112:2).

- My children are taught of the Lord and great is their peace (Isaiah 54:13).

- The Word of God is a lamp to my children's feet and a light that directs their paths (Psalm 119:105).

- In the name of Jesus, I declare that their lives are redeemed from destruction, sickness, debt, poverty and death (Isaiah 54:14).

- God has given His angels charge over my children to keep them in all their ways (Psalm 91:11). No weapon formed against them prospers (Isaiah 54:17).

- My children increase in every area of life—spirit, soul, body and finances (Psalm 115:14; Luke 2:52).

- Every need in my children's lives is met (Philippians 4:19).

- My children walk in the favor of God and man (Psalm 5:12).

- My sons have the spirit of Joseph and they are successful in all that they do (Genesis 39:2). I declare that my daughters are virtuous according to Proverbs 31.

- I declare that goodness and mercy follow my children all the days of their lives. (Psalm 23:6).

- My words have creative ability (Proverbs 18:21), and in the name of Jesus, I have what I say. I release most holy faith to bring these things to pass. Father, Your Word says, *"Let the redeemed of the Lord say so..."* (Psalm 107:2). Therefore, I declare these things to be so now, and I receive them in Jesus' name, Amen.

2

DAILY
CONFESSIONS FOR
HUSBANDS

Developing Character

- In the name of Jesus, I declare that I am a man of God. I am righteous, godly, faithful, loving, patient and meek (1 Timothy 6:11).

- I am perfected by God's Word and am thoroughly equipped for every good work (2 Timothy 3:17).

- The Word of God is a lamp to my feet and a light that directs my path (Psalm 119:105).

- The wisdom of God is formed within me and it directs me in every area of my life (Proverbs 3:6; Colossians 1:9; 3:16).

- I allow the Holy Spirit to lead me down the path toward the good life (Ephesians 2:10, *AMP*).

- I declare that my mind is renewed by God's Word (Romans 12:2). As a result, I am able to experience the "good life" (Ephesians 2:10, *AMP*).

- I know God's perfect will for me, and I walk worthy of the Lord and His calling on my life. I please Him and am fruitful in every good work (Colossians 1:9-10).

- I have put off the old man and put on the new, which is renewed in the knowledge of Him Who created me (Colossians 3:10).

- God's plan for me includes prosperity in every area of my life—spirit, soul, body and finances (Psalm 35:27; 1 Thessalonians 5:23; 3 John 2).

- I possess the power to get wealth, and I declare that today is my day to receive financial abundance (Deuteronomy 8:18).

- I speak to the mountains of insufficiency, sickness and debt, and I command them to be removed from my life right now (Mark 11:23).

- I declare that God's expected end for me does not include evil, but His peace (Jeremiah 29:11).

- I understand the purpose for the anointing on my life and do not abuse it (Isaiah 10:27; Luke 4:18; Acts 10:38).

A Happy and Healthy Home Life

- God prospers and provides for me; therefore, I am able to provide for my household (1 Timothy 5:8).

- I honor God by honoring my family.

- I am the head of my home and I lead it with godliness and temperance (Ephesians 5:23; 1 Peter 1:5-6).

- My entire household is saved and serves the Lord (Joshua 24:15; Acts 16:31).

- Our lives are redeemed from the curse of destruction, sickness, poverty, debt and death (Isaiah 54:14, 17).

- I choose to love my wife as Christ loves the Church by giving her first place and consideration in all that I do. I avoid anger, bitterness and strife at all costs (Ephesians 5:25; Colossians 3:19).

- In loving my wife, I love myself (Ephesians 5:28).

- My wife is a virtuous woman; she is my crown. I trust and submit to her and she trusts and submits to me (Proverbs 12:4; 31:11; Ephesians 5:21).

- I will not allow any corrupt communication to proceed out of my mouth toward my wife, but only that which is good for edifying so that my words minister grace to her (Ephesians 4:29). I only speak words that encourage my wife in her walk of faith.

- I give my wife the honor, respect, goodwill and kindness that is due her (1 Corinthians 7:3).

- We are one in Jesus Christ, the Anointed One and His Anointing (Genesis 2:24; Ephesians 5:31).

- As I increase in the knowledge of God, my marriage is made strong (Colossians 1:9).

- Alone, I can put 1,000 to flight; however, when my wife and I are in agreement, we can put 10,000 to flight (Deuteronomy 32:30). Therefore, I make a decision to stand in agreement with her.

- My wife and I exercise the power of agreement and live in constant victory (Matthew 18:19).

- God has joined us together and no one can separate or defeat us (Matthew 19:6; Mark 10:9).

Building Healthy In-Law Relationships

- I love my in-laws and do not enter into strife with them (Proverbs 10:12).

- Thank You, Father, for giving me in-laws that are saved, sanctified and filled with the Holy Ghost.

- I declare that nobody but Jesus sits on the throne of their lives, and because Jesus sits there, my in-laws have love, joy, peace and prosperity in the Holy Ghost (Galatians 5:22).

- They are born of God and love me with His Love (1 John 4:7).

- The Spirit of the Lord rests on my in-laws and they provide me with godly counsel and wisdom regarding family matters (Isaiah 11:2).

- My words have creative ability (Proverbs 18:21), and in the name of Jesus, I have what I say. I release most holy faith to bring these things to pass. Father, Your Word says, *"Let the redeemed of the Lord say so…"* (Psalm 107:2). Therefore, I declare these things to be so now, and I receive them in Jesus' name, Amen.

3

DAILY
CONFESSIONS FOR
WIVES

Developing Character

- In the name of Jesus, I declare that I am a virtuous woman of God. I am a woman of moral excellence and strength (Proverbs 31:17, 25).

- I reverentially fear the Lord. I desire to have the favor of God on my life more than that of man (Proverbs 31:30).

- I constantly renew my mind to the Word of God, taking on the mind of Christ. Apart from Him I can do nothing (Romans 12:2; John 15:5).

- I desire the sincere milk of the Word so that I grow in the things of God (1 Peter 2:2).

- I take good care of my body because it is the temple of the Holy Spirit. I exercise, get the proper amount of sleep and eat nutritious meals. Because of this, I am able to look after my husband and family (1 Corinthians 6:19-20).

- I know God's perfect will for my life, and I walk in a manner that is worthy of the Lord. I am fruitful in every good work (Colossians 1:9-10).

- I manage my household with godly wisdom (1 Corinthians 2:16).

- I keep God's commandments and abide in His love (John 15:10). Therefore, my home is filled with God's love.

- I possess the power to get wealth (Deuteronomy 8:18). I am a money magnet; money comes to me.

- I handle the household money wisely because I seek first the counsel of God and that of my husband (Proverbs 31:16).

- I do not waste precious time by being idle. I take care of all that needs taking care of in a timely and efficient manner (Proverbs 31:27; Ephesians 5:16).

- In the name of Jesus, I speak to the mountains of insufficiency, sickness and debt and I command them to be removed from my life and my family's life right now (Mark 11:23).

- I represent God; therefore, I dress appropriately because I am a godly woman and I have self-respect. I maintain a clean and attractive appearance (1 Timothy 2:9).

- I submit myself wholly to my husband, for this pleases the Lord (Ephesians 5:22-24).

- My husband trusts me. He can rely on me for wise counsel (Proverbs 31:11).

- Proverbs 18:22 says that the man who finds a wife finds a good thing. In addition, he obtains favor from God. Therefore, I declare that I am a benefit, and not a burden, to my husband.

- I operate in the anointing, which is the burden-removing, yoke-destroying power of God (Isaiah 10:27). I am empowered with wisdom to resolve challenges because He gives me ideas, concepts and inventions (Proverbs 8:12).

- I am the righteousness of God (Romans 3:22). As such, I have the right to come boldly before His throne and receive answers to my prayers.

- Because I am righteous, I am perfected by God's Word (Psalm 138:8) and thoroughly equipped for all good works (2 Timothy 3:17).

- I am a wise, understanding and prudent wife. I conduct the affairs of my household with wisdom. The Word says that houses and wealth are inherited from parents, but only the Lord can provide a wife (Proverbs 19:14).

- I first take care of my husband and family and then reach out to others in need (Proverbs 31:20).

- I obey the Word of God; therefore, wealth and riches are in my house. My obedience brings provision (Deuteronomy 8:1, 18; Psalm 112:3).

Characteristics of a Godly Husband

- In the name of Jesus, I declare that my husband is saved and serves the Lord (Joshua 24:15; Acts 16:31).

- I love, honor and respect my spouse and speak well of him to others. I speak kindly to him for his edification (Proverbs 31:26).

- My husband is faithful to me. He has no need to go elsewhere, because I provide everything he needs and desires (Proverbs 5:18-19).

- I was created to be a suitable helpmate for my husband. Everything he needs is in me. He lacks no good thing (Proverbs 31:12).

- My husband loves me as Christ loves the church. He has left his mother and father and cleaves only to me. We are one (Ephesians 5:25, 31).

- I declare that my husband's life is redeemed from destruction and that no weapon formed against him prospers (Isaiah 54:17).

- My husband is a mighty man of valor and protects, provides and leads our family in the perfect will of God for our lives (Judges 6:12).

- God perfects those things that concern my husband (Psalm 138:8).

- My spouse handles money wisely. He is careful to pay tithes and offerings and give firstfruits (Malachi 3:8-11; Romans 11:16). Because of this, the windows of heaven remain open over our lives. God rebukes the devourer for our sake because we are faithful with the tithe.

- My husband no longer thinks like the world. He renews his mind daily with the Word of God (Romans 12:2).

- The Word of God is a lamp to my husband's feet. As a result, he guides our family with wisdom and has the power to obtain wealth (Psalm 119:105; Deuteronomy 8:18).

- Because my husband is obedient to God's commandments, his days shall be long on the earth. He also has peace, or wholeness, in every area of his life. There is nothing missing, lacking or broken (Proverbs 3:1-2).

- My husband is blessed because I am like a fruitful vine. Our children are like olive plants around our table (Psalm 128:3).

- My husband provides abundantly for our family as a direct result of God providing abundantly for him (1 Timothy 5:8).

- My husband is the undisputed head of our household and he leads with godliness and temperance (Ephesians 5:23; 1 Peter 5:6).

Building Healthy In-Law Relationships

- Thank You, Father, for giving me in-laws that are saved and filled with the Holy Spirit.

- I declare that nobody but Jesus sits on the throne of their lives, and because Jesus sits there, my in-laws have love, joy, peace and prosperity in the Holy Spirit (Galatians 5:22).

- They are born of God and love me with His love (1 John 4:7).

- I love my in-laws and do not enter into strife with them (Proverbs 10:12).

- The Spirit of the Lord rests on my in-laws and they provide me with godly counsel and wisdom regarding family matters (Isaiah 11:2).

- My words have creative ability (Proverbs 18:21), and in the name of Jesus, I have what I say. I release most holy faith to bring these things to pass. Father, Your Word says, "*Let the redeemed of the Lord say so...*" (Psalm 107:2). Therefore, I declare these things to be so now, and I receive them in Jesus' name, Amen.

4

DAILY
CONFESSIONS FOR
TEENS

Developing Faith in the Word

- I know that the Word of God is the will of God, and when I pray according to His will, He hears my prayers and confessions. As a result, I have high levels of confidence and expectation, because I know that God will give me whatever I ask of Him (1 John 5:14-15).

- My words have the power to bring life to me. Therefore, I choose to speak words of life and not death (Proverbs 18:21).

- I declare, according to Romans 3:3-4, that God's Word is true. I accept it as the true and final authority in my life. I do not accept what man says unless it agrees with God's Word. I am fully convinced that God is able to do what He has promised in His Word (Romans 4:21).

- I know that when I obey God's Word, it gives me direction and brings about change in my life. His Word is able to keep every thing in my life going well.

- I don't neglect the promises of God by concentrating on my problems (Romans 4:20). I always keep God's Word on my tongue. My faith is strong like Abraham's.

- According to Galatians 5:6, my faith begins to work when I walk in love. Jesus said that if I love Him I will keep His Word (John 14:15). I cause my faith to work by obeying the Word of God.

Faithfulness to God

- I love the Lord my God with all my heart, soul, mind and strength, and I love others as myself (Luke 10:27).

- I declare that the Lord defends me because I seek Him wholeheartedly (Jeremiah 29:13).

- I declare that the Lord rewards me because I seek Him diligently (Hebrews 11:6).

- I have control over every situation I face because I seek God first in all that I do.

- Psalm 42:1-2 says: "*As the deer thirsts for water…My soul thirsts for God…*" (*NKJV*) Because I hunger and thirst for righteousness (right-standing), I shall be filled (Matthew 5:6).

God's Love

- I believe, according to Jeremiah 31:3, that the Lord loves me with an everlasting love.

- God's love always thinks the best of me. I am secure in His love because I know He desires to give me the best (Jeremiah 29:11). God's love toward me is unconditional and limitless. According to Romans 8:38-39, nothing shall separate me from it.

- I declare that the Lord loves me and rejoices over me daily (Jeremiah 32:41).

- I am able to love God because He first loved me (1 John 4:19).

- God loves me so much that He does not remember anything I have done wrong (Hebrews 10:17).

Excellent Academic Performance

- I declare, according to Proverbs 28:5, that because I seek the Lord first concerning my studies, I understand my assignments and do well in all subjects.

- I have the wisdom of God; therefore, no lesson is too difficult for me to understand. God teaches me everything I need to know concerning my schoolwork.

- I have a greater understanding of my schoolwork because I constantly think about what God has done for me.

- I do as God's Word commands and study to show myself approved (2 Timothy 2:15).

- I am wise because I surround myself with wise people (Proverbs 13:20).

- My diligent study habits are always rewarded (Proverbs 10:4).

Overcoming Lust and Abstaining From Fornication

- My body was not made to participate in any kind of sexual activity outside of marriage; instead, it was made to glorify God (1 Corinthians 6:13-20). My body belongs to Him because He purchased it with the blood of Jesus. As a result, the Holy Spirit lives inside of me, and I am one with the Father.

- I choose not to look at anyone in a lustful way (Matthew 5:28). I know how to abstain from sexual sin and honor God with my body (1 Thessalonians 4:3-4).

- I do not damage or destroy my soul (my mind, will and emotions) by fornicating (Proverbs 6:32). Neither do I go places or associate with people who tempt me to have premarital sex (Proverbs 7:7-8).

- I allow the wisdom and knowledge of God to control my thoughts so I can avoid the immoral people who try to seduce me (Proverbs 2:10,16).

- I guard my heart and mind by meditating on God's Word. I will not allow any immoral thoughts to stay in my mind. Instead, I cast down every thought that is contrary to God's Word by declaring the Word over that situation. I do not look to the right or to the left, but straight ahead to the Word of God (Proverbs 4:23-27; 2 Corinthians 10:4-5).

- I will not allow fornication to prevent me from inheriting the Kingdom of God (Proverbs 6:32-33; 7:27; Ephesians 5:5; Galatians 5:19-21).

- I do not live according to the desires of my flesh. Through the power of the Holy Spirit, I put to death the evil desires of my flesh and fill my heart with God's Word.

DAILY CONFESSIONS FOR TEENS

Getting the Most Out of Church

- I faithfully attend church services and participate in teen ministry. I am eager to attend every time the doors are open (Hebrews 10:25).

- I pay attention to my pastor and youth pastor when they give instructions from God's Word. I will allow their words to give direction to my life (Jeremiah 3:15).

- My ears are anointed to hear and I understand what is being taught when I am listening to the Word of God (Matthew 13:16).

- I am attentive to God's Word when it is being taught (Proverbs 4:20-22). I speak to my body now and say, "Body, you will not fall asleep, but will hear every word that is spoken."

Choosing Good Friends

- I choose my friends carefully, and I am not led astray by the ways of the wicked (Proverbs 12:26).

- I declare that my friends and I love each other at all times (Proverbs 17:17).

- According to Ecclesiastes 4:9-12, I have friends who help me when I am in need. I also help them in their time of need.

- I do not establish friendships with people who do not agree with my decision to obey God's Word. (1Corinthians 1:10; Philippians 1:27; 2:2; 2 Corinthians 6:14-18).

- I have friends because I am friendly to others (Proverbs 18:24).

Developing Boldness to Stand Up for What's Right

- I let no one think less of me because I am young. I declare that I have the boldness to stand up for what is right, and I am an example for my peers (1 Timothy 4:12, *AMP*).

- According to 2 Corinthians 5:21, I am the righteousness of God in Christ Jesus, the Anointed One. Therefore, I am as bold as a lion (Proverbs 28:1).

- I am strong and courageous. I do not look to the right or to the left for strength, but only to Almighty God (Joshua 1:6-7). My strength comes from the Lord; as a result, I have good success.

- Just as God gave Peter and John the boldness to speak His Word, He has also given me the boldness to confess Jesus openly before all men (Acts 4:29).

- I am not ashamed of the Gospel of Jesus, the Anointed One, for it is the power of God (Romans 1:16).

Safety in School,
the Community and at Home

- Although hard times may come, they pass me by because I am established in righteousness (Isaiah 54:14-15). No weapon formed against me prospers (Isaiah 54:17).

- I fear no evil because God is with me. The Word of God and the Holy Spirit comfort me (Psalm 23). Greater is He who is in me than he who is in the world (1 John 4:4).

- Because I abide in God and He abides in me, He is my refuge. In Him I put my trust. God always delivers me from the person attempting to trap me (Psalm 91:1-5).

- I am not afraid of anything. Thousands may fall around me, but nothing evil comes near me (Psalm 91:5-10).

- Because I have set my love on God and know the authority that is in His Word, I declare that I have the right to call on Him and receive answers to my prayers (Psalm 91:14-16). The Almighty is with me when trouble comes. He delivers me and honors me with His goodness and mercy. I will not die an early death, but will experience a long, peaceful and satisfying life.

Overcoming Alcohol, Tobacco and Drugs

- I do not allow myself to consume any alcohol or illegal drug (Proverbs 20:1).

- According to 1 Peter 2:9, I am royalty; therefore, I will not allow myself to ever forget what God is doing for and through me. I refuse to allow alcohol and drugs to cause me to forget the judgment of God (Proverbs 31:4-5).

- According to Ecclesiastes 10:17, I have full control of my body. I do not allow *lasciviousness*, or a lack of restraint, to come into my life.

- I do not allow myself to become addicted to alcohol; instead, I remember the work of the Lord in my life and in the lives of others (Isaiah 5:11-13).

- I cast my cares on God because He cares for me (1 Peter 5:7). As a result, I never have to use alcohol, tobacco or illegal drugs as an escape to avoid facing my problems.

- According to Ephesians 5:18, I am filled with the Holy Ghost.

Overcoming Peer Pressure

- According to 2 Corinthians 5:21, I am the righteousness of God in Christ. This is where my identity is found—in God and not in people (Proverbs 13:6).

- I walk with wise people; therefore, I am wise. I am not a friend to fools; therefore, I shall not be destroyed by foolish decisions (Proverbs 13:20).

- I do not give in when sinners tempt me to go astray from God's standards (Proverbs 1:10).

- I allow the wisdom of God to enter into my heart and thinking (Proverbs 2:10-13). As a result, discretion and understanding preserve me. I avoid the way of evil and the man who speaks against God.

- I honor my parents as I do the Lord, because it guarantees me a long and satisfying life (Ephesians 6:1-3). I walk by faith and not by sight (Hebrews 11: 6).

Concerning the Use of Profanity

- I do not allow any corrupt communication to come out of my mouth, but only that which is encouraging for others to hear (Ephesians 4:29).

- I do not allow filthy communication to come out of my mouth because it corrupts good manners. I put off the old man and take on the characteristics of the new one (Colossians 3: 8-9; 1 Corinthians 15:33).

- I refuse to allow both good (praise) and evil (cursing) words to come out of my mouth, because this is not right. I only allow good things to come forth (James 3:9-12).

Being the Best in Life

- I will never give myself over to an easy or convenient path. I diligently walk the path God has ordained for me. I shall never lack anything, because I am constantly putting my hand to work. I will experience abundance because of my faithfulness to the things of God (Proverbs 6: 6-11; 10:4, 24; 13:4; 21:5, 17).

- I declare that I have an excellent spirit—one that constantly strives to be and do better (Daniel 6:3). As a result, I receive continual promotion and favor from God.

- I walk in understanding (Proverbs 17:27). Because I seek the Lord first in everything I do, I understand everything (Proverbs 28:5).

- I am not a sluggard (Proverbs 13:4), and I shall not remain unfulfilled. Instead, I am diligent and will be made rich.

- My thoughts are centered only on abundance (Proverbs 21:5). I am not hasty, but cautious and observant. As such, I do not lack any good thing.

- My words have creative ability (Proverbs 18:21), and in the name of Jesus, I have what I say. I release most holy faith to bring these things to pass in my life. Be it unto me according to my faith. In Jesus' name, Amen.